# THE TERRORIST AT MY TABLE

**Imtiaz Dharker** grew up a Muslim Calvinist in a Lahori household in Glasgow, was adopted by India and married into Wales. She is an accomplished artist and documentary film-maker, and has published six collections with Bloodaxe in Britain, all including her own drawings: *Postcards from god* [including *Purdah*] (1997), *I speak for the devil* (2001), *The terrorist at my table* (2006) *Leaving Fingerprints* (2009), *Over the Moon* (2014) and *Luck is the Hook* (2018). She was awarded the Queen's Gold Medal for Poetry 2014.

# IMTIAZ DHARKER

# The terrorist at my table

BLOODAXE BOOKS

Poems & drawings copyright © Imtiaz Dharker 2006

ISBN: 978 1 85224 735 5

First published 2006 by
Bloodaxe Books Ltd,
Eastburn,
South Park,
Hexham,
Northumberland NE46 1BS.

Reprinted 2012, 2015, 2019, 2023

**www.bloodaxebooks.com**
For further information about Bloodaxe titles
please visit our website or write to
the above address for a catalogue.

Supported using public funding by
**ARTS COUNCIL
ENGLAND**

Printed in Great Britain by Bell & Bain Limited, Glasgow, Scotland, on
acid-free paper sourced from mills with FSC chain of custody certification.

*For Simon*

# ACKNOWLEDGEMENTS

The poems in 'Remember Andalus' were first broadcast in the programme *Another Country* by BBC Radio 4.

'Call' was written as part of *Phone Home*, BBC Radio 3.

Poems from the sequence 'Lascar Johnnie' were broadcast in *The Strange and Violent Case of Mr Biswas*, BBC Radio 3.

'Glass house', 'Dreams', 'Tow-path', 'Ragpicker', 'Hung', 'Nazar na lage', 'Myth', 'Black and white', 'Before' and 'If' were commissioned as part of the programme *With Love from Me to You*, BBC Radio 4.

A version of 'These are the times we live in' first appeared in the British Council magazine and the complete sequence was published in *The Statesman*, Calcutta.

'Sari' was first published in *Out of Fashion, an anthology of poems*, edited by Carol Ann Duffy (Faber, 2004).

The cover drawing by Imtiaz Dharker is in the collection of Smita and Rahul Bhatnagar, Hong Kong.

# CONTENTS

## 3. WORLD RICKSHAW RIDE

# 1

# THE TERRORIST AT MY TABLE

# The terrorist at my table

# Tissue

Paper that lets the light
shine through, this
is what could alter things.
Paper thinned by age or touching,

the kind you find in well-used books,
the back of the Koran, where a hand
has written in the names and histories,
who was born to whom,

the height and weight, who
died where and how, on which sepia date,
pages smoothed and stroked and turned
transparent with attention.

If buildings were paper, I might
feel their drift, see how easily
they fall away on a sigh, a shift
in the direction of the wind.

Maps too. The sun shines through
their borderlines, the marks
that rivers make, roads,
railtracks, mountainfolds,

Fine slips from grocery shops
that say how much was sold
and what was paid by credit card
might fly our lives like paper kites.

An architect could use all this,
place layer over layer, luminous
script over numbers over line,
and never wish to build again with brick

or block, but let the daylight break
through capitals and monoliths,
through the shapes that pride can make,
find a way to trace a grand design

with living tissue, raise a structure
never meant to last,
of paper smoothed and stroked
and thinned to be transparent,

turned into your skin.

## Mine. Yours.

Whose news do you receive here?
The same image comes
with different words.

I pick up a piece of mud,
hold it in my fist,
and call it mine.
You put your foot here,
pick up the same piece
of mud and call it yours.

This mud is my grandmother,
grandfather, mother, father.
This mud is my feast days
and my celebrations
my food, my animals, my grain.
It is my songs and dances.
I tell you this for years.
You say it is too late.
You say this mud is your sons and daughters
and their children, your sweat and blood
your cities and your orange groves
the pain you carried through so many centuries,
your prayers.

When did a handful of mud
turn to god?
When did sod
turn to promised land?
We are standing at the beginning
of what has already happened.

Do you have cable here?
Which channels do you get?
Is it our news or yours?

Perhaps one of them will tell us,
using the same words
and the same names,
who we killed today.

# My breath

Walls are paper.
Have you ever listened through them

for my breath? Do you remember
the shape it used to have

inside my body?
It is impatient now

to be let out, sent on its way
by courier perhaps, sped away

on highways from village into town
as if it were a message

that could matter to someone.
My breathing is calmer

now that the need is simplified
to seeing another dawn.

You are waving to me.
My neighbour is lighting a fire.

Woodsmoke makes everything real
as if the world has shifted back,

shivered into the shape
it used to have

before they made new maps,
before the documents changed hands.

# Translations

Can you translate my hands and feet?

I am the heat rising
off your rooftop at midday.
Perhaps you recognise
my pulse inside the song,
silence, surprise,
passed along from mouth to grain.

Boots have beaten out a change
of seasons, overtaken
the promise of fruit trees
and driven back the harvest.
I have adapted to change.

With every choice lifted away
simplicity remains
Today I am alive. Today
we are still here.
Today my children
have eaten. Today there was
water. Praise God.

These things mean the same
in my language or in yours.

But how will you translate my mouth?

# Its face

A woman getting on a plane.
This is how it will happen.
A bird that has stopped singing
on a still road. This is how it will sound.

This cloth belongs to my face.
Who pulled it off?

That day I saw you
as if a window had broken.
Sharp, with edges that could cut
through cloth and skin.

You wrapped my mouth in plastic
and told me to breathe in free air.
This is how it will feel.

I remember heroes.
Figs, dates, a mango.
This food, your enemy's food.
This is how it will taste.

It will not come
slouching out of the ground.
It walks along a street
that has a familiar name.

This is how it will look.
It will have my face.

# The terrorist at my table

I slice sentences to turn them into
onions. On this chopping board, they
seem more organised,
as if with a little effort
I could begin
to understand their shape.

At my back, the news is the same
as usual. A train
blown up, hostages taken.
Outside, in Pollokshields, the rain.

I go upstairs, come down.
I go to the kitchen.
When things are in their place,
they look less difficult.
I cut and chop. I don't need to see,
through onion tears,
my own hand power the knife.

Here is the food. I put it on the table.
The tablecloth is fine cutwork,
sent from home. Beneath it, Gaza
is a spreading watermark.

Here are the facts, fine
as onion rings.
The same ones can come chopped
or sliced.

Shoes, kitchens, onions can be left
behind, but at a price.
Knowledge is something you can choose
to give away,
but giving and taking leave a stain.

Who gave the gift of Palestine?

Cut this. Chop this,
this delicate thing
haloed in onion skin.

Your generosity turns my hands
to knives,
the tablecloth to fire.

Outside, on the face of Jerusalem,
I feel the rain.

# The right word

Outside the door,
lurking in the shadows,
is a terrorist.

Is that the wrong description?
Outside that door,
taking shelter in the shadows,
is a freedom-fighter.

I haven't got this right.
Outside, waiting in the shadows,
is a hostile militant.

Are words no more
than waving, wavering flags?
Outside your door,
watchful in the shadows,
is a guerrilla warrior.

God help me.
Outside, defying every shadow,
stands a martyr.
I saw his face.

No words can help me now.
Just outside the door,
lost in shadows,
is a child who looks like mine.

One word for you.
Outside my door,
his hand too steady,
his eyes too hard
is a boy who looks like your son, too.

I open the door.
Come in, I say.
Come in and eat with us.

The child steps in
and carefully, at my door,
takes off his shoes.

# Platform

On the platform opposite
three men and one woman
are reading newspapers,
six people are speaking into phones,
or listening. One is sitting on a tin
case marked 'Fragile'.
A boy yawns, then
looks at the girl wearing green boots.

The board shuffles
through its pack of numbers.
A poster offers Escape Routes.
Trains come and go.

Now only four on phones.
Where did that man
go, carrying his fragile cargo?
Easy to lose count.
Some leave in time. Some stay.

## Almost

I launch myself into
the fabric of this city. It refolds
itself around me, a face
where the expressions
are about to change. That road

is a frown, that square
a smile, that garden an open eye
that pulls birds in.

All of this has made itself as if
it were a poem. On the shifting
lifeline of its road, I will need
to reread its disconnected lines.

The details are beyond
me.

It is the face I once
imagined, but imagined
incomplete.

# Campsie Fells

What did we look like?
A band of gypsies
set free out of solid homes
for one Sunday morning,
catapulted into the countryside,
a caravan.
All the families, Auntie Ameena,
Uncle Ramzan, a variety of children
in flowered frocks and wide shalwars,
clothes that responded to the wind.

What were we like, on that
Scottish field, up in the hills,
navigating the cow-pats,
paddling in sweet streams?

The children made daisy chains.
Azaan
shone a buttercup beneath our chins
to check if we loved butter.

And when the picnic was opened out,
the competition began, between
the families.
Who brought boiled eggs and sandwiches,
who made kebabs and tikkas with chutney.
The thermos flasks of tea,
all made up with sugar and with milk.

My mother settled like a queen,
a sculpture, took possession of that field,
spread all her goods around her.

The green sharpened.
The sun always blazed,
The long evenings never grew cold.

The Aunties began to speak
about old films, *Alvida, Alvida*
sang bits of songs
that always sounded sad,
*Tum bhi kho gaye, hum bhi kho gaye.*
Lines of remembered poems
made Uncle Asif cry.
Azaan asked, 'If you mind so much,
why don't you go back?'

Uncle Asif, wiping his eyes, replied,
'Our families are scattered. My brothers
and their wives are here. The village has changed.
My uncles have moved to town.
I'm not sure if anyone knows us any more.
And would you go get Zenab
out of the cow-shit and wash your hands
before you touch those chips?'

Afterwards we washed the cups.
Our names splashed in the stream,
no questions asked.

# Azaan

Azaan still carries a school-bag
but he calls it 'rucksack'
and slings it like the beginning of a revolution
on his shoulder.

It pulls the shirt-collar away
from his pale neck,
and I have to stop myself
from leaning over, and touching the nape,
the 'V' of baby hair.

He skids more than moves,
slouches sideways when he walks.
Speaks in monosyllables,
if he does at all.

I heard him laugh
yesterday, though,
when he was watching
the evening news.

## Sound as a pound

It was at the football. Just
someone being friendly,
standing up for me.

A man began to shout,
no reason, and this person
came over. The man went away.

It wasn't about politics.
Life is short enough.
It wasn't anything the maulvi said.
No one lectured me

or told me what to do.
No one tried to mess with my head.
I wasn't looking for a pass to Paradise.

It wasn't about God and stuff.

I just felt stronger
with my friend around.
On solid ground.

# Who made me?

Who put a gun in my hand
and took away my land
Who made me?
Who took my mouth
and put it behind a mask,
who offered me democracy,
who set me free?

Who put the leeches on my back?
Who bled me?
Who told me I should follow them?
Who led me?

Who stroked my head,
sang me to sleep,
Who fed me?

Whose hand should I bite?
Who made me?

# Firm

Here I am, standing at a window on the thirtieth floor,
looking down.
I feel the strength and power
of this place, the shafts of steel
soaring like angels' wings
to lift me up.
Great slabs of concrete, every block
down to the foundations, locked
into the ground,
air conditioning ducts, electric wiring
all to raise me up.
No gusts of wind can shake it.
My feet are firmly planted here.

Secure.

This building has windows
that make the shape
of a list.

I am on the thirtieth floor,
fifteen windows
from the left. Can you see me
from up there, from

that plane?

# Text

I am sending a message again.
Maybe you can't hear it
through all the noise of lights
and the dangerous way things move
in that other city
where I think you are,
if I have the dates right, though
of course I could be wrong.

If you expected the message,
you would stand like this,
with your eyes open and focussed
on the screen, your ears closed.

The city I am in has lost
its volume control.
Every person in the place
is tuned to maximum.

Can you see the text?
Just to ask if you are safe
and well?

A phone shrills, a clock explodes,
in the next room, a TV switches on.
Everywhere, the sound of sirens, drills.
Cars screech, horns blare.

Where
are you?
Why have you stopped singing?

# Hung

We are suspended above the street,
twelve floors up, nine clouds down,
north of the river, south of peace.
Beneath our feet the city is blossoming
with wet umbrellas on living stalks,
men and women on business
less concrete than poppies.

We float without time.
The whole of London is our present,
sent to us in battered envelopes
postmarked Srinagar, Ramallah, Grozny.
Torn free, the pieces tumble out,
shreds of something we have known
ever since we read the name
in other countries, in second-hand books.
Familiar street signs,
parts of jigsawed parks
posted, received, patched together at last.

The world set out below us grows
closer every day. This has become
our neighbourhood,
these our neighbours.

Those feet
we hear hurrying over
Southwark bridge or down a Kabul street
belong to people we know

people we expect to meet.

# Before I

This is what was happening
before the planes came in.
She woke early,

switched on the songs,
fetched milk and put it on to heat.
Bare feet slapped across the floor.

She shook the children awake,
her voice a little hoarse
from sleep.

She was thinking about
what she would pack
for them to eat

at school, something
cooling in the heat.
And now, the water.

The water spilling
out of a steel glass.

All this happened
before.

# Before  II

A broken desk. A name carved in,
a script I do not understand.

Clock hands are having to move
backwards, to wipe their faces clean.

I will keep standing here,
where it happened, in the wrong place.

We could all stand here
where it happened, until it comes right.

My hands are picking at the threads
of streets that need mending.

Could you send back the messages,
unwrite them, and turn the television off?

The beds we slept in, shattered,
begin to remake themselves.

Sheets spread again,
smoothed down, white again.

Desks and chairs reform,
find their small comfortable scars.

The children get up off the floor
and sit as they were

before

# Still

I was not abused.
There was no torture.

I never wore a hood,
or stood on that box,

a noose around my neck.
They never leashed

me, or made me crawl
on all fours across

the prison floor. All
the more surprising, then,

that these welts have
risen on my back,

appeared on throat and wrist.
I was in a clean, warm house

nowhere near that war.
But in my fist the paper

crumples to embrace
the photograph. The woman

laughing for the camera,
pointing at my face.

# Black and white

All the people are wearing black.
Coming out of stations, scrambling
on buses, crossing the street, stacked
on escalators

they look like letters running away
from words I am stuggling to understand.
There is no way to fix them
blurred as they are by movement,
mirrors and cracked glass.

I am trying to write you down
on this white space
in longhand, calm
you, still you,
put my arms around you,
touch your face, trace
the cheekbone,
hold you long enough
for you to read

the words we have been assembling.

# If

If we could pray. If
we could say we have come here

together, to grow into a tree,
if we could see our blue hands

holding up the moon, and hear
how small the sound is

when it slips through
our fingers into water,

when the meaning of words melts
away and sugarcane speaks

in fields more clearly
than our tongues,

when a child takes
a stick as long as itself

and rolls a wheel
down a lane on wings of dust,

in control, would we
think then that we should thank

someone? If we knew
we could turn, and turning

feel that things could be different.
But we are unused

to gratitude, if we could lose
our pride, bend down

look for peace on the iron
ground. If we could

kneel

These are the times we live in

# Dramatic breakthrough makes for gripping television

Two suspects edge slowly from the front door of a ... flat and into the ... ...armed ... third-storey ... laser-guided sights of ... police. Shirtless and spitting, perhaps from the gas used to flush them out, and they stand defenceless with their arms stretched out on the balcony wall.

After a siege which lasted several hours, they even suffer the indignity of a commonplace nightmare: appearing in public without trousers. As a precaution they had been forced to partially strip by police.

It was gripping footage and

floor flat had been at large and considered by police as highly dangerous. In a few moments they would be captured, a key part of the most profitable day yet in the hunt ... the would-be suicide bombers.

The footage could not have been planned better by a professional director. The camera was steady, the focus sharp and the walkway access design of the flat even provided a stage for the action.

As the two men emerged from the flat the executives at ITV News and the Daily Mail knew they had a remarkable scoop. Having snapped up the rights to

footage shot by an amateur from a neighbouring flat, they plastered every frame with the word "exclusive".

Police had pulled the plug on the rolling news channels as the operation reached its climax, but not before viewers saw police dramatically ... ...rers of armour.

...
pulling on ...
Gripping though that was, it was eclipsed by the denouement.

Until last night's broadcast, the hunt for the July 21 suspects had been played out through a shadowy and frustrating collage of blurred CCTV footage, mobile phone film clips and grainy screen grabs. Londoners' fears that

the fugitives could strike again were compounded by the murky imagery which seemed to make their personalities and motives so frustratingly mysterious.

But just eight days after the attack here we were, watching suspects exposed in crystal clear television pictures. The rapid transition from ... ...meras to ... grainy security ... this daylight clarity summed up the incredible speed of this police investigation.

A cameo role was played by two children who emerged from their front door on the floor below, curiosity aroused by a policeman dressed in body armour and a helmet ...

44

# These are the times we live in   I

You hand over your passport. He
looks at your face and starts
reading you backwards from the last page.
You could be offended,
but in the end, you decide
it makes as much sense
as anything else,
given the times we live in.

You shrink to the size
of the book in his hand.
You can see his mind working:
Keep an eye on that name.
It contains a Z, and it just moved house.
The birthmark shifted recently
to another arm or leg.
Nothing is quite the same
as it should be.
But what do you expect?
It's a sign of the times we live in.

In front of you,
he flicks to the photograph,
and looks at you suspiciously.

That's when you really have to laugh.
While you were flying,
up in the air
they changed your chin
and redid your hair.
They scrubbed out your mouth
and rubbed out your eyes.
They made you over completely.

And all that's left is his look of surprise,
because you don't match your photograph.
Even that is coming apart.

The pieces are there
but they missed out your heart.

Half your face splits away,
drifts on to the page of a newspaper
that's dated today.

It rustles as it lands.

## These are the times we live in  II

Fight to get out of this.
Wrestle your way through.
Stop this thing
that is happening to you.
I'm nobody, you must say.
Don't point me out,
erase my photograph.
My name can't be on the list.
I wasn't on that plane,
that bus, that train,
I had left the building.

I don't belong inside
your cage of coverage.
I'm not in the news.
Get me out of here,
you say
I still have everything to lose.

## These are the times we live in  III

They got an eraser as big as a house
and they began to use it to delete your life,
the names of your lanes and roads and streets,
your stories and your histories,
your lullabies. They rubbed
out your truth, and they left in your lies.
They snatched your family portraits,
shot them all over again with different people,
started from scratch.
They took your books and broke their backs
cracked their spines,
the margins gone, all the lines
jumbled together, pages torn.

Your words have packed their bags
and gone. New ones have crawled
back
all crumpled
and small
like jailbirds
into cages,
to fit
the times
we live in.

# Open

People are running
through my body now,
calling out, laughing,
some singing.

Strange for someone as secretive
as me, I don't mind.
I'm opening up the public spaces.
There are no intruders.
They own this place as much as you,
as much as me.

My arms are more relaxed now,
no tension in the neck.
Lately, I've fallen into a new habit,

leaving my life unlocked.

## The Password

You have to remember the Password.
Without it you can't get in
to anything you think you own.

Just try to remember.
Is it your birth date?
The day we met?
The name of your first lover
maiden name of your mother
your first poem
the mythical figure, your favourite song?
The city, the village, the road
where you belong?

Give it to me.
Right now.
Wrong!
You don't have the Password.
That was your last try. Sorry.
Pack up. Move on. Goodbye.

## Still here

You look at yourself in mirrors,
in panes of glass dimmed to black,
in shop-windows when the lights are off,
in bits of chrome on cars,

Your glance catches and sticks
to every surface
that holds even
a hope of a reflection.

I know what it is:
Not vanity.
Its just to reassure yourself
you are still in place.

Still here.

# Ragpicker

I may set myself up
at the edge of this city,
one of those people, stooped,
who wait to see what will wash up
out of waves of traffic and feet,
collecting, a ragpicker.

I will make
a note of the shapes of things
when they fall off the edge,
take in the flotsam
escaped from the nets
of passing lives.

A scrap of newspaper, a broken
glass bangle, a soft-drink tin,
a plastic bottle, coconut husk,
someone's shoe, a carrier bag, everything
you would expect to find
on its way to a garbage bin.

These will be my precious
artefacts, left from when the world
was normal, worth saving,
putting in glass cases,
on pedestals, lit up
by halogen,

annotated.
People will stop, peer
in. Look at this, they will say,

They did this.
They lived like this.

# Lascar Johnnie 1930

*In the 1930s, twenty percent of Britain's maritime labour force was made up of Indian seamen, called Lascars. Many stayed on at ports like Glasgow, some as itinerant salesmen, peddling their wares in remote parts of Scotland.*

# Lascar

I am invisible, in a ship manned
by invisible men, hands without names.
The captain does not see us,
but there are times when the ship does,
when it forgets its cargo of cotton,
loses its grip on sugar and tobacco,
and reshapes itself around its living load.

This is when it lifts a little
and the water slips
into the road I travel every night,
cradled by sugarcane, overhung
with tamarind. The air
has the sting of the songs we sing,
sharp with the taste of Jhelum.

Water cannot satisfy my tongue.
My thirst needs broad Punjabi,
my feet scrabble for flat earth, the plains.
Sometimes leaving America,
sometimes coming in to Glasgow,
I see another shoreline, sprung
with palms.

The captain chooses not to hear
our songs, or know our names.
Allahuddin, Mohammed, Mubarak, Bismillah.
Our names are prayers.
Someone must be saying them tonight
in the other country

like a conversation, as if we were there.

# Glasgow, shore leave

Ten o'clock, and still light.
This city, when I land, hands
me a gift of unexpected hours,
feeding them like sweetmeats
into my unanchored life.

So different this, that
for a moment I miss
nothing, streets and seas away
from sunset at six, the lamps
lighting up bright mud and clay.

Here instead, a day
offered like an unbroken egg,
still alive with possibility,
a long pause for thought
between last light

and night. Women lean out
over window-sills
and washing hung on lines,
to shout across to other women.
Between tenement

and tenement, words jostle home
like buffaloes. I know
the feel of this language.
It has big bony hips, and corners
that could bruise your lips.
One woman calls out to another.
Then they laugh.

Inside me, when I look,
it is still light.

# Close

I'll tell you, I was like you once, not
knowing where to go or what
to do. In a place where no one
speaks your tongue you are a child again.

See, go up from the dock,
turn left, then right, too many streets
to tell, you might
find a countryman to ask.

It may be hard to see, this time
of night, but when you reach the close
go up the stairs to the seamen's mission,
top floor, I think three flights.

Then it is our own country.
People from our village
giving proper food and rice,
sometimes, God willing, a bed.

If you are fortunate enough to sleep,
the bed becomes a charpoy
that takes you home
to just outside your door.

And in the dawn, when you wake,
balanced between light and shade,
there is dew on your body
and woodsmoke begins to fold the stars away.

# Johnnie

Between villages, a long way.
Longer between houses,

Each one nothing but a small square
of light behind the next hill

and the next, a trudge
from one year to the next.

The cardboard suitcase collects
another brick with every step.

Sometimes I knock and no one
answers.

Sometimes a curtain lifts,
dropping warmth on my side of the wall.

When I speak, my breath
hangs up a curtain of its own.

I hold out cotton, show her pinnies, smile,
speak up quickly, Bargain, Missus.

She takes one, maybe out of kindness,
gives me a cup of tea with milk.

Whit's yer name, son? I make it
easy for her. Johnnie.

She pays. Two pennies Missus.
As I go, she smiles.

# Jaan

Doorway. On the step, my wares
laid out, everything I have,
my life laid bare.

Doorstep. A woman doubtfully
fingers cloth, and shakes her head.
Too dear, Johnnie.

Doorway. Standing there, my wife,
jasmine in her hair, called me
Jaan, her life.

Doorstep. When
will you come home, Jaanu?
How will I cut my days?

You know how it is.
Someone says your name.
Jaan. John. Jaanu. Johnnie.

Your head turns, too quickly.
Your eyes expect
another doorway

another kind of light.

# The right way

You call this
tea?
Black brew, no sugar, raw milk?
Let me tell you how it should be.
Put the water in the pan.
Add sugar, more than that,
more. Then boil it
till it becomes quite syrupy.
Now add the tea-leaves,
let them boil, to get
your money's worth from them.
This is when
my wife would put in
ginger, cinnamon, or seeds of cardamom.
You have none of those?
No matter, let me show you.
Put milk now. Boil again,
yes, boil. Let it rise,
turn down the heat.
Turn it up, let it rise again,
sizzling. Blow on it to keep it
bubbling just inside the rim.
This takes skill, and shows respect
to both tea and guest.

Then take the cup
and strain it in. No,
don't drink yet,
I am showing you the way
we drink tea in my village.

Pour it in
to the saucer, blow.
Now drink. Don't shake, don't spill.
Don't laugh.
Good, no?

# 'Remember Andalus'

OSAMA BIN LADEN

*'Culture is a form of memory against effacement'*

EDWARD SAID

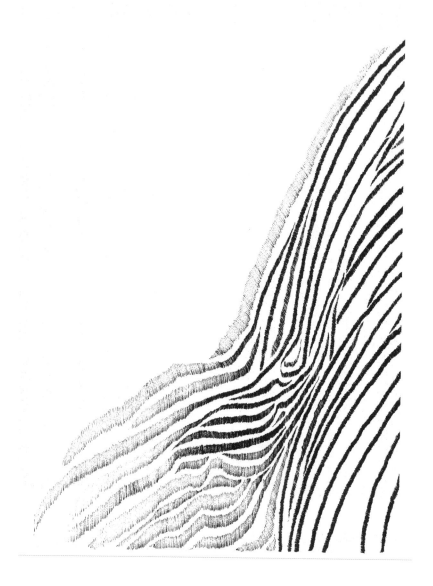

# Alif, Anar

It was a whole idea of life
concentrated into one thing,
wrapped in tissue paper.

My mother and father carried
it home, the kind of gift
the magi might bring,
bought off a barrow, out
of the bitter Glasgow rain.

They came in laughing
at the pleasure of squandering
a shilling on it.

Her hand went
to the big brown paper bag,
her smile mysterious.
She handed it to him.

Tissue paper rustled.
Then, he produced the prize
that made the room
rearrange itself, sit up.

'Look, Anar!'
He lifted it in his hand,
strange fruit, shining.
Back to Alif.
The opening

# How to cut a pomegranate

'Never,' said my father,
'Never cut a pomegranate
through the heart. It will weep blood.
Treat it delicately, with respect.

Just slit the upper skin across four quarters.
This is a magic fruit,
so when you split it open, be prepared
for the jewels of the world to tumble out,
more precious than garnets,
more lustrous than rubies,
lit as if from inside.
Each jewel contains a living seed.
Separate one crystal.
Hold it up to catch the light.
Inside is a whole universe.
No common jewel can give you this.'

Afterwards, I tried to make necklaces
of pomegranate seeds.
The juice spurted out, bright crimson,
and stained my fingers, then my mouth.

I didn't mind. The juice tasted of gardens
I had never seen, voluptuous
with myrtle, lemon, jasmine,
and alive with parrots' wings.

The pomegranate reminded me
that somewhere I had another home.

# Train to Granada

Endless plains simmer
past the windows of this train.
I have crossed hours of rough landscape,
the whole length of Spain
to reach this place.

Was I mistaken? Not a train
but a cavalcade, thundering in
to Andalus on Arabian horses,
heading towards the hill
where room by room
they would carve out a quiet space.

The sun glints off helmets, polished steel,
shields, coats of mail.
Their momentum lifts the stream of banners
they would prefer to leave behind.

At last the plains begin to stir,
lift themselves into folds like faces,
roll themselves up into small, rounded hills.

These hills have the look
of miniatures,
the kind of landscape the artist meant to keep
in the background of the main event.

For them,
the hint of a fuller, softer life.

Tired of war and threats,
looking for a safe haven,
peace, a promise of rest,
a hope of poetry.

# Inside

Inside the architects make arabesques,
delicate columns to hold up
the mathematicians' model of heaven
caught between hands and walls.

Not carved from marble, not gold
but brightness trapped in simple plaster,
with no claim on eternity.
They pour light into inner spaces.
They open windows to their ambition,
every garden a map of paradise
engineered with a precise longing,
to channel rain down from the mountains,
play it through water courses,
fountains, ornamental pools,
as if it were a song.

Song turned liquid,
soil made sumptuous,

the secret,
the jewel inside the fruit.

# Women bathing

All our lives, in every city,
out of every landscape
the waters of the Alhambra
have been murmuring to us.
From fountains, from watercourses,
from the secret pools in courtyards,
voices calling across centuries.

The other women are bathing
in the moonlight.

'Come,' they say, 'Come out of the day's heat,
out of shaded rooms, let's escape and slip away,
let the veils fall, one by one.
Slide into the pools that lie like mirrors of the sky,
and let the moon wash over our bodies.'

Bodies lush, generously-hipped.
Bodies like pomegranates,
bursting with promises.

# The women

I scatter pomegranate seeds,
and from each seed springs a woman.

There is the one who sits
in the window, day and night,
rapt in the life on the opposite hill.

There is the one who slips out
into the garden, and comes
back with her hair undone.

And I am on my way to meet them,

just one more seed,
flung a little further than the rest.

# Aixa at the window

There is no other time
when exactly this will happen.
My standing here
at the fortress window,
more a slit of concentration
than a window,
more a skin than a barricade.

Inside is Paradise.

But I am watching, from another century,
tenses changing on the opposite hill.

I lean out to hear
the voices from the bazaar, pitched high,
each one distinct, speaking in my ear.

I listen to their haggling,
laugh at their jokes,
taste their sweet mint tea, clink glass on glass,
hear all their bustling,
coming, going, up and down the hill.

And the sounds float back.
The click of heels,
the singing from a future century.
Songs from films with dancing heroines.
Songs from MTV
laid like tissue over finer tissue,
they find my mouth,
whisper out of me.

# What the women said

WOMAN 1:  Wait, let me see your face.
          Why are you hurrying out of the garden?
WOMAN 2:  Why is your hair loose and wild?
WOMAN 3:  What's chasing you?
WOMAN 4:  Why are you out of breath?
WOMAN 5:  What is that purple stain on your neck,
          like a bruise on fruit?

# Aixa at the Alhambra

It wasn't the man. It was the garden
that seduced me. The breeze
glanced off the white mountains
and blew secret messages to me.

I looked at the pomegranate blossoms
and they blushed.
The leaves on all the myrtles
shivered when I passed
and I suspected they felt what I felt.

Out of deep shade, oranges winked at me.
Flowers turned to look. I felt adored.

Then the cypresses began to speak to me.
I came to understand
every lift of leaf and turn of limb
quite intimately.

Birds came to my fingers and nibbled there.

The sun stretched over
groves of lemon trees.
The sun suggested I'd be cooler
if I took off one veil,
then another.

Fountains whispered.
From the pool in the courtyard,
the water invited me in.
Don't be afraid, the water said,
it won't hurt a bit,
and gently, gently slipped over my body,
water fingers, water tongues.

Then I ate a pomegranate.
The juice stained my skin.

This garden is out of control now.
A garden rampant.
It grew and grew and grew right into me.

Today a bee stung my mouth.

I know you think it was him.
But it was just the garden, all along.

# What the moon saw

The moon is lying in the pool,
quite still.
I offer it a toe,
which it licks, shivering
just a little,

I could choose to stay
outside.
I could decide to slip
in.

Was that an accident?
That I dropped my veil?

# What the water knows

This is how it is to travel.
The real journey slides in and out
of imagined ones,
the idea of a place,
the waking dreams.
This history is real,
this one supposed.

Andalus was open doors,
a conversation between equal voices,
a poem made with simple words.

These things will not be trapped
in marble, the moon in water
has never been the same before or since.
No one, in any age, will be
what Aixa is. The women are
unrepeatable, each one has her
history, her own mole or tic.

The trick is to remember this,
to build with stucco, knowing it will fall,
to cherish the ephemeral.

The princess watches a girl
wash clothes on a terrace
of the Albayzin. The water
will never fall like this again.
The clothes are hanging out to dry.
There is a red T-shirt, a pair of jeans.
She looks from one century,
across to another century on the opposite hill.

Tomorrow is drawing pictures
inside her
with the hands of a child.

# The last sigh

Galleries and courtyards, high terraces,
barbican walls, red towers
set like a jewel upon the hill,
the white spine of mountains,
the city spread below...

Gone.

Murmuring watercourses, fountains,
pools, sheets of sky lying on the ground,
a million singing birds,
orange trees and flowers,
the scent of jasmine...

All gone from me.

Poems, words, the beauty of a turn of phrase...

All blown away,

Ballads, songs of love, roundelays...

Not a whisper now.

I gave up a key.
I gave up every wall and window,
every memory.

And this is all
I can lay claim to:

Hands that hold a key
of empty air.
A body that houses nothing
but my breath.

Breath that comes and goes
as if it were a visitor.

They will say I looked back
from the Hill of Tears
on a winter morning.
Only they will not see my breath,
left like a mist on Paradise.

I will know I left my breath behind.

They will say I sighed.

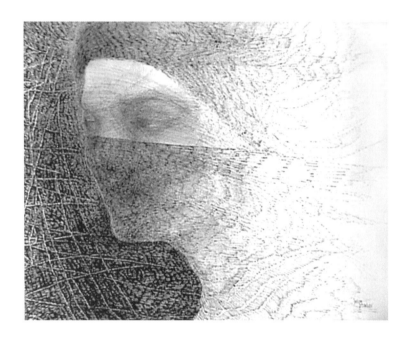

# 2

# THE HABIT OF DEPARTURE

# Light

Every single light was on.
That's what I remember
when you told me
on the phone,

your voice flat, folded in
against the news.
It would all begin again,
the daily studying of cells,
your real life picked and pressed
between the pages of before and after,
tracks to and from the hospital.
Dropping into tissued veins,
the carefully measured grams of hope.

I remember looking up
and counting,
as if it could change something,
as if a book could open
and find illumination.

Six halogens,
four outside the window,
two lights through
frosted glass.

There was too much light.
The night passed

# Never trust the daffodils

He distrusts daffodils
and is especially wary of crocuses.
Traitors of hope, he says,
they promise spring
and callously deceive you
into optimism.

He has learned to question
the ordinariness of things,
never to stroll in
with his hands in his pockets,
whistling.

He has learned the hard way
to be pleasantly surprised
when the frost forgets
to come up from behind and bite.

He turns his back, moves on.

Green shoots break through
the winter clods of earth.
Against his better judgement,
his shoulders feel
the touch of spring.

# Mersey crossing

Small boy, red knees and nose,
sharp knuckles on the rail, you crossed

from Pierhead to New Brighton,
there and back and back again.

You folded up whole days
between two riverbanks,

half your mind on the rivermouth,
the north and west, the east and south,

the whole world wide for you
and out of breath.

Today, on the river
whose ships have sailed away,

grey waves sliding over darker grey,
you point to places I must see

when you are not there,
some other day.

The whole city, the grand sweep
of buildings from an earlier, confident time,

the lights just coming on,
the riverflow, the sky, all seem

to lean in towards you
as I do

to take warmth
from the shelter that you make

against a bitter wind.
It seems the natural way of things.

Some other day
I will unwrap your life to look

at what you have become,
far flung,

spread out to north and south,
beyond the rivermouth,

but blessed with a small boy's
stubbornness.

Between the riverbanks, obsessed
with finding,

always crossing, crossing,
crossing back again.

# Captive

You went out the other day,
caught a city like a bird for me,
and put it in a window-frame
to amuse me in my captivity

Revisiting the prison door
is risky. Opening it is the start
of certain madness.
Inside the frame and outside,
separated by it and yet joined,
we watch each other
with no means to hide
how much we change.

Light passes through our canyons,
skies wheel, traffic moves
across our face,
the face we share, reflected
in each other's glass.

Chance has put us here.
Chance keeps us here,
two willing captives,
the city and I,
given to each other
like a gift.

Don't open the door too soon.
Among the electric trees,
across a transparent moon
we are spinning fragile monuments
to celebrate ourselves.

We are still here, still alive.

# Carving

Others can carve out
their space
in tombs and pyramids.
Our time cannot be trapped
in cages.
Nor hope, nor laughter.
We let the moment rise
like birds and planes and angels
to the sky.

Eternity is this.
Your breath on the window-pane,
living walls with shining eyes.
The surprise of spires,
uncompromising verticals. Knowing
we have been spared
to lift our faces up
for one more day,
into one more sunrise.

# Off the ground

So this is how you grew.
In a house stirred up
with wings, dragonflies,
birdmobiles, butterflies,
magic horses, paradise
carpets, imaginings,

things your mother drew
into her orbit. She
calls it a muddle. Everything
flies around her
in a happy flurry, nothing
anchored down, all
with the air of being about
to flit out through
the window, wheeling
round across the poppies,
to pluck fish out˙of the pond.

What you chose
to carry with you was the pools
of colour,

reset now
with the fine eye of an architect,
put down at a precise angle.
in another place,
but still with the tilt
of something on the brink
of departure.
These colours are thinking of flight.

That's how I see you,
always on the point of setting off,
hovering,
only one foot on the ground.

# Walk

And as we walk, the river rushes
through our day. We have begun
to count these seasons in seconds.
Spring has turned, on a single gust of wind,
to leaves running with us through the park.

We see people we have passed before,
and they become our stories, partly told.

Summer is a plan for bluebells
we will plant under the birch trees
in the Vale of Clwyd
to mix with the scent
of wild garlic.

In your hand, my hand warms itself.

Frost on the broad walk
holds our breath up to the world
for admiration,
still hung out over the morning
in some other time
where I am waiting
for you to wake.

# Tow-path

Every step we take
could have been a step
in another direction.
This time we choose
to go to the canal.
By the time we reach it
the day decides to stop
following us around.

While we are picking
our way down, watching our feet,
the park packs up, the city
moves a few miles away.
Children's voices are balloons
released to open sky.
Behind us footsteps fade,
streets turn into water.

Leaf by leaf, the day
grows smaller. Whoever we are now,
this has been bequeathed to us.
Every other claimant has stepped aside.
Our steps the only steps.
The last finger of light points out
landmarks we do not recognise.

Still, between the cobbled banks,
cradled by bare branches.
we know we will be safe.
Now, even the unknown path
will tow us home.

# Up

Suddenly, Camden.
A shock of garish voices
flaunting black as if
it were red or purple, feathered,
sequined, weaving
on the lock one perfect,
glittering peacock eye.

Across the bridge,
a dustier tapestry of leaves,
the water sewn through
with floating orange peel,
eggshells, plastic cups.

We climb up through Islington,
behind the supermarket mall,
then back to the canal.
It has more secrets up its sleeve.

The city's generous arms
open to accommodate
marinas, boats hidden like toys
under the coats of trees.

A morning walk changes to late evening.
Sometimes you give up my hand,
fall behind to let a cyclist pass,
and when I turn to look at you,
at the jewelled lip of water,

you smile like someone with another
secret up another sleeve.

# Accepted offerings

These are the offerings to the water.

A bronze elephant god
with four small hands and a big
paunch, found at Little Venice.

A few fish-hooks, an iron bangle,
a topaz brooch with one jewel gone,
a can of Coke and empty
lager tins, adrift at Islington.

A monkey god minus a leg
but still in flight, holding
up a mountain.
A sodden prayer-mat near St Paul's,
a kirpan found near Albert Bridge.

A leather book-cover with
no book. What kind of gods
accept these assorted things?

A cross made of silver
at Regent's Park canal,
a syringe, a plastic wallet
with the image
of a haloed saint.

Dented paper cups as well.
All offered. All taken
by the willing water.

# Dreams

I write down his dreams,
pulled in to the sleeping
and waking of his night,
punctuated by the light switched on,
switched off.

They had to look around to find
the vein that would be strong enough
to hold the dreams
they were going to put in, the people
he would gather up and take with him
along a stream
of country roads that lead
to unknown
imagined towns, polished cities,
squares in civil geometry.

My blood turns round with his
till we break through, into the clearing
of his heart, and stop, amazed,
struck by light, the sight
of tables laid, glasses he has filled,
making, dreaming, waking
to unexpected wine.

## Castings nets

There is an old woman sitting on a bench.
She comes every day to sit on this bench,
every day like a patient fisherwoman, casting nets
into the sea of passers-by.
We pass by, we pass this way,
we pass her by, and every day
we see a bench. Old women are invisible.

Fish don't see the fisherwoman, they see
the bait. We pass. She waits.
She casts another net.
We forget that we have passed this way.
At times around us we feel
the shimmer of the shoal.
At night in bed the blue net flickers over us.
In the net the shape of fish
but no fish.

She waits for us all night.
All night we swim into her sight,
the shape of us waiting to be filled,
the flicker of recognition
in her familiar eyes.

# Nazar na lage

Like a mother in some village
in Gujarat or Maharashtra
who puts a black mark on her baby's cheek
to soften the blow of its beauty,
like a woman who knows
anything can change, and will,
like someone in daily contact
with the power of gods
and neighbours,

like one who loves a thing
too much,
I take ash on my thumb
to leave on your forehead
my stain of disbelief.

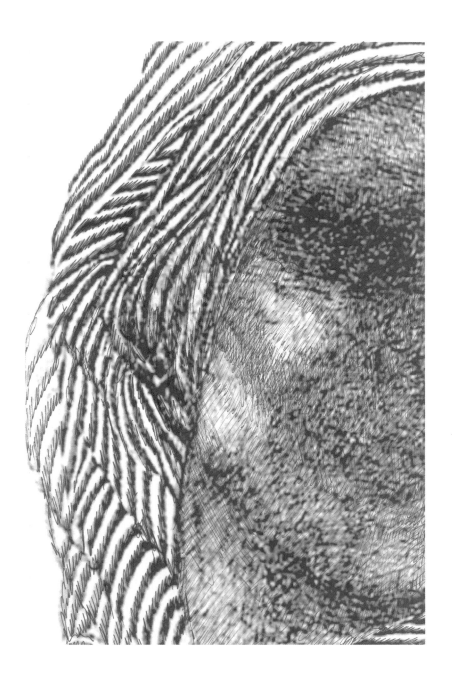

# Opaque

Why are these clothes
such solid, unrelenting things?

Who dictated they should be
opaque?

Where did they get the right
to fight my outlines?

Why should they have weight?
Don't I have any say?

Weave me a dress of light,
a net made out of blue

switched on like
runways in the dawn

to say to you
as you circle the sky

Touch down.
This is the way.

# In camera

A camera will tell me what I did.
It will record the movements,
the walk through streets,
the corner café and the moment
when the sun rose or set
and where I went to eat, to talk,
drink wine.

A camera will tell me what I said,
while the world was turning,
elections happening, typhoons raging
somewhere else.
It will say I spoke
to this friend or that,
that I told a story, badly.

A camera will tell me
what I did not do or say.
It will tell me you were not in the frame.
It will show me streets you never walked in.
It will show me empty chairs,
your glass of wine
untouched.

## I need

I need *sarson da saag*,
nothing else will satisfy me,

and hot *makki di roti*
with butter melting over it.

I need to eat bacon and eggs
and the petals off a rose, one by one.

My greed has no nationality.
I need my mother's chicken *salan*.

I want her to break the *roti*
scoop up the gravy

and keep putting it in my mouth
until my hunger's done.

I need to run
out to my father's land

and sit in the *ganna* field
where I can hear the sugar growing,

juice rushing up through the stem
to reach my waiting mouth.

I need to tear the outer skin
and crunch the sugar-veins.

I am hungry to be the woman
watching the young man

bathing at the well,
water running down his back,

streaming down the length
of his black, black hair.

I need to crack walnuts with my teeth
and eat their brains.

I need to take a train
to somewhere, and get off

at platforms I don't know
to drink sweet milky tea

steaming in the early morning
out of earthen *khullars.*

I need to go to Crawford Market
through the piles of fruit

and buy a whole sack
of ripe mangoes

to suck and suck
till nothing is left but dry seeds.

I need you to come back.

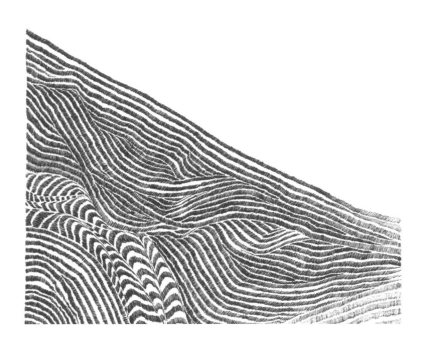

# Inspiration

The poet tells me he needs to hide
in the hills in solitude to write.
He says nothing comes to him
through sounds of traffic,
no words can penetrate
the turbulence of a city night.

Give me railway stations.
Voices on loudspeakers,
people with their surfaces pulled away
by travelling. Movement gives me words,
carried in the carriages of trains.

Give me a tea-stall on a busy street,
halves of conversations,
stories walking by.

I will not go with my friend
the poet to the mountains.
Stillness lives inside the poem,
not out.

# Thrown away

They come back sometimes, by mistake,
the lost, forgotten poems.
On the backs of estimates
for furniture, behind grocery bills,
black scribbles laid over fine print.
The ones on envelopes, of course,
keep turning up,
others fallen off the edge of maps.
Hardest to keep are the ones
written on paper napkins
with the name of the café
in one corner, bottom right,
the kind you could use so easily
to blow your nose,
and throw away.

Some go because they don't
deserve to stay.

Is there a place where all
the lost words go?
Poems crumpled into balls and
tossed in wastepaper-bins,
poems left behind on trains,
poems flown into the wind,

a litter of kisses blown
on to your cheek,
that you have felt
and brushed away?

# Sari

The street stretches its back.
Its spine cracks with satisfaction.

There's no bustle, no sense of rush,
just the determined slip and slap
of soap on slate
and cloth on stone,
morning light thrashed out
on the wet step
above the water-tank.

Her arm an arc, her haunch
pushed back,
the whole length of sari
thwacked.
Legs apart, she attacks
the sweat of yesterday,
the cooking smells,
the dribble from the baby's mouth,
drives them out
of thin and daily thinning cloth.

Today she wears the orange,
washes green,
tosses it out to dry,
smacks it down across the stones
like an accomplishment
of fine clean weave.

Sun and light break through.
Through and through,
her day begun.

The city rolls its hip,
picks up its plastic bucket,
walks away.

# Woman on a train

The woman on the train
is cutting vegetables, bhindi
for the night, something that
will cook quickly, just right
for after she gets home.

Her fingers slightly green
from okra juice, glutinous strings
turn her into a puppet-master,
the vegetables her puppets.

Ladies' fingers, they call them,
elegant and pointed, slightly
curved, now chopped.

She looks around, stops,
comes back to me. I look away.
She goes back to cutting, looks at me
again. Is there something
she wants to say? Some
urgent matter distracting her
from the task at hand?

She finishes the last stem,
then, as if it were a continuation
of her chore, puts out her hand,
tucks in my bra-strap
surveys the vegetables
in her lap with satisfaction.
*Accha,*
*that's done*, she says.

# Where her sari hangs

Over the window-sill,
dead still. Below it
empty pots and buckets
clatter, trucks roar,
brakes shriek, buses rip
through a city driven mad by heat.
Tight streets
hold their breath.

Sudden, sweet, echoing through
the flame of the forest, a sound
from another century,
a koel sings, a promise
that the rain will come.

The smell of the earth will change,
lovers will be filled
with longing, one will sing,
another will hum
on separate balconies,
perhaps the same song.
A million tin roofs will sizzle
and turn into a giant drum.

Not yet.
For now, all that happens is
the sari stirs,
takes a deep breath,
lifts.

# Maxwell Park

*(for Shahnaz)*


Your shadow is longer than mine.
At three foot nothing, a long way

to Maxwell Park, in unaccustomed
heat, and identical

summer dresses, full of flowers,
flared from the high waist

and the smocking. Too small
for stockings, white socks

rolled at the ankle,
and bows on our bunches.

A hot shilling in my hand
down the hill at Bruce Road,

I keep asking, 'Will there be
Ice Poles? Can I buy sweeties?'

But you have something else
in mind. You don't answer.

At the park gates, everything
changes, goes quiet,

our shadows have pointed the way
to your secret,

where voices are purple
and heads have haloes.

I'm whispering now
'Where are the sweeties?'

You point under the trees
to where we are heading,

under the blue shadowed trees,
the bluebells.

# I would come this way again

Birling and birling harder, this is the way
we girls make the world around us whirl
until it turns into an O! of admiration.
Hands locked, wrists crossed,
a scurry of hot toes,
our poppy-printed cotton frocks
furling and unfurling,
liberated into parachutes.

Turning and turning, summer days
stretch their long fingers
through our hair, arcs fanned out
and twirled about, tossed free
of nylon bows. The earth tilts
under us. This is when buttons pop
and shoe-straps snap
and our ankle-socks grow wings.

Spinning and spinning,
lifted out of patent shoes,
our feet have lost us, trip us,
trap us in a curl of laughing,
girls unwrapped,
birling and birling,
all of Glasgow stirred
around the wild commotion of our hair.

# Flood
*(for Neil Astley)*


Did I imagine the water flooding
the track, under the wheels at York?
Leaving the train with all the others
spilt out into the rain,
and buses to Durham?

Tracks turn to rivers,
rivers gone mad,
towns taken by storm,
green turned to excess
and streets roiling over.

Through the thunder
and the boiling sky,
cathedral bells run wild
and the choir shifts an octave
higher

past miles of columns, to arches
that point the heart upward.

Out of stuffy showrooms,
even the furniture is set free.
A sofa in yellow leather
escapes its station in life,
abandons its pomp, shows

its true colours.
In a rush of madness
sofa unbound,
sofa magnificent
dances away downstream

high on water
and the organ's joyful sound.

116

# Out of place
*(for Sally, Ty Newydd)*

The wind swept her towards us,
unwrapped from fields,
and over her shoulder
the busy Criccieth sea,
holding not the flowers
or shells we might expect to see,
but this, an onion.

Shining,
bursting out of its gold papery skin,
mysterious thing.

She shifted it to her left hand,
shook ours, looked
at it, as if she had surprised herself.

'How absurd,' she said.
'An onion. A phone call from my father.
He needed one.'

'My father too,' I almost say,
even though he is four thousand miles away.

'First,' my mother always said,
'Fry onions. The smell of it
will bring them in.'
The family drawn like fish
to the big table.

Somewhere, in his empty house,
the phone rings.

In her hands,
my gift
to him.

# Call

So many voices, throwing floodlights
on our lives.
My hand shields the phone.
After all the clatter and the shouting
I stand alone, in the small space
made by the candle that is your voice,
trying to open a window back to home.

Everywhere, the noise,
the sound of tills, traffic,
sirens, electric drills.
Even the birdsong
has a different accent,
hustling the day along.
I came here to stand still,
after weeks of hesitating
at other people's doors,
seeing their lives in lighted windows,
looking in at basements, at dinner
being made, smelling the food,
all the tables laid.

I measure out your voice in seconds.

I have rung to see
if our tamarind tree is still there,
where my brothers are,
because home moved house
to bring me here,
and faces crumpled with the years.
Fields shifted
further and closer with the drift
of light and shade, and the seasons
made different clothes for me,

heavy, weighed down by wool.
And you are sitting alone
in a room in a house in another country.

# The blue wall

The blue wall
has seen it all, but
is not cynical.
Every time it blinks
something changes
as if a code has broken
to change it into another thing.

The soul shrinks and grows.
Window and mirror
are alive with sky.
Light blossoms out of distant songs.
Cloth flutters off
the fleeting gold
that may be skin.
A woman comes close
to the brink
of revelation

and all this time
the blue wall thinks
of nothing
but the taste of oranges

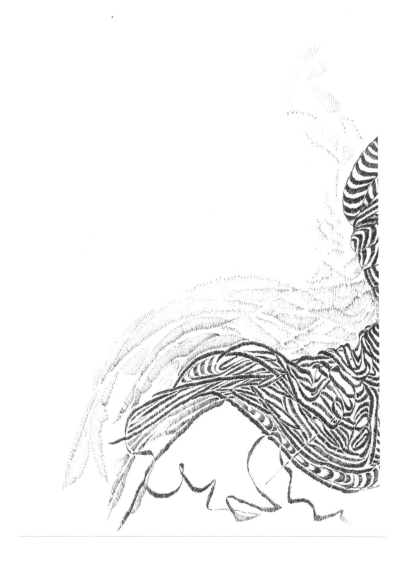

# Glass house

The room I choose to live in
is a bowl of glass.
I look out. People look in.
Feel free,
I have no secrets
you shouldn't see, there are
no skeletons here, no one else's head
inside my bed,
just me.

Aquarium light spills
off the leaves, slides in,
touches my walls with silver green,
shifting with the shade and sun.
My whole life floats
inches off the ground,

Goldfish in a greenish bowl.
My room is swimming,
lit up from inside my head.

Here. Look through me.

# Snail's pace

It starts slow and ends slow
sucks itself along the flagstones
you can try to stop it
but its antennae are up
it's on its way
past the rivulets of monsoon rain
over muddy hillocks and pebbles
past faster rats and pushing things
the light from a window slanting down
across the shell of its troublesome home
where it feels the light and the world
and you
it can feel where you are
it is watching
but slowly
wet trail on the stone
it can smell your skin
its longing clings to you
inches along
past gutters and ditches
past stars and constellations of stars
past singing and arias
this thought
this snail
this patient waiting

and it is slow but it will not stop

# 3

# WORLD RICKSHAW RIDE

the landmarks the landmarks the land
are blurred blurred blurred blurred bl
urred blurred blurred blurred blu
blurred blurred blurred blurred blur

# Rickshaw rider

I can see the face
of the man at the wheel
who's making my bones
feel every bump in the road
as we reel around corners
and thump over stones.

Mad rickshaw driver, my life
in his hands, his hands
a gorilla's steering us through
the markets at Mulund
Malad and Kandivali, Khar
and Borivali to Bandra Bandstand.

Phut phuting fast forward
in spite of his bulk, floor
bucking, doorless, Bajaj autorickshaw,
on three crazy wheels
tuk tuking along to a dhinchak song,
and the horn, the horn.

Mahim flies past.
I open my mouth to
remind him this isn't allowed
but a crowd of policemen
wave him right on, winking
and laughing.

The landmarks are blurred
and the meter is ticking
when the one-eyed driver
lets out a laugh and wheels grab air.
The real world is a road
that hobbles away from beneath us.

Whole sentences walk out
of the place where I'm sitting
puffing and sweating
stuck tight in the fright
and the heat to the back
of my rexine seat.

He chugs out past seabirds,
past the port, onwards over
the Arabian sea. I try
to catch his one eye
in the mirror but he's hunched
over the wheel.

He's over Karachi, Clifton
down there, my eye latches on
to anything static, a building,
a stone. I ask him a question
but the wind grabs it out
of my mouth and it's gone,

lost in our sputtering
puttering wake. My whole life
is history. By any standards
we're not moving fast,
not like an Enfield,
not even at Ambassador speed

but unstoppable, with a kind of a
hop
and a kick in the wheels,
a laugh in the face
of a world gone mad.
I steal a look at him in the mirror.

A Cyclops in motion
A hulk on the screen,
he's seen every angle and been
many things to many people,
and if he has a mind
it's his own.

On the windshield
a string of plastic jasmine jumps
up an down with excitement.
Far below, I see the world shrug.
One more mad rickshaw.
So tell me what's new?

# Dug in

Tell me what's new?
Anything with foundations
dug deep underground, planted.
Anything solid, anything that stands
still.

Down there, someone
is digging a hole, planning to build
something made to stand
firm.

I can hear this sound.
The excavator's rough grunt
comes to grips with ground,
rips.

Its claw lifts.
In its fingernails, earth,
roots, plastic, hair, bone,
worm.

The claw turns it around,
considers it,
grins.

This needs to be explained.

# Red ribbons

This needs to be explained,

a strange recurrence,

this one girl we pass
again and again
coming out of the makeshift hut
at the end of every dusty street.

It could be
the red ribbons that she wears,
shining against the careful hair,
nylon formed into a perfect bow,
plumped out and backlit by the sun.
The one
who emerges out of chaos,
poised. Just so.

How many of her are there?
How many, stepping out of the door,
coming out of the alleyway?
The one who strides down dirt tracks,
The one who has filled an ocean,
bucket by bucket, all her power
concentrated in the hip-bone,
the arm at work,
pulling in the socket.

How many steps will take her
to the well?
How many steps before she draws
the line?

# Glass

Draw that line.
Draw a line on all the footsteps

from home to water,
from water back to home.

Now draw those lines again
across her face,

the woman striding down
a city street.

This is how faces look
after they have broken through

partitions, ceilings, walls,
seductive cloth, gold

cages, curtains of fire.
Wired hard to light

the kind that whips
the darkness off the soul

unties the knotted heart,
ties bright ribbons in her hair

and makes her body whole

# Rickshaw driver

Her body whole by a hair's breadth,
the girl crosses the street
in front of us.
He swerves.
When he does I see his eye,
empty.

*Koi fikr nahin*,
Nothing to worry, he says,
We missed.

He blows his horn.
After a while he says,
These roads are different
since I was last here. They feel
much tighter now.

I clear my throat.

Then he asks,
casually,
Do you know the way?

# Mogul driver

*It is said that the media mogul Rupert Murdoch,*
*enchanted by the Bombay autorickshaw,*
*captured one and carried it away to Hong Kong.*


This is the way
it happened. The media mogul
fell madly in love with the rickshaw,
completely *fida*.
He wooed it, wired it, sent it
flowers, spent hours reading poems
and singing ghazals to it,
won it over.

You can see why.
This thing can take you anywhere
over a huge footprint,
over the air.

This thing has attitude
that's jaw-dropping
breath-stopping

# Cave

Breath stops at the edge
of comprehension.

The makers of this,
faced with the muscle and weight

of the gods they hunted
and ate each day,

found power in a line
of charcoal, a slash of manganese.

The nearness of death
makes them matter-of-fact

in the act of forgiveness,
where they set a trap

deep below the fields
and purple forests

for the beast with the hoof
and the horn and the claw,

a door to strange worship
with cunning and crayons

to capture
in line and paint
the master, this god.

# The Driver's Domain

A godlike footprint, Japan
to the Middle East. The beast
takes on new bodies,
tiger, lion. The mogul learns
quickly. What goes down well
in Singapore is gibberish
in Sri Lanka.

Holding hands with Beijing. All's fair
in love, and the magnate is mad in love.
He sprays his heart out of cans
all over the walls of Tiananmen Square,
graffiti spread across continents,
a truly global love affair.

He owns every shade
of news, from pink to green to blue.
A mouse in the hand, he rides
his creatures, draws with light
on a million screens,
every day enslaved, the footprint
branded on his forehead,
he believes himself a king.

In another time and another domain,
a hand is working
against the dark, making pictures
on a rock wall with charcoal,
manganese, the precious flame
a bison that could not be tamed.

There is a point to this.

# His reach

The point of light becomes a screen
switched on. The boy's face is washed
blue in the light.

On the train, a woman is
reading about asylum.
Sunlight squats on the platform.

Another satellite dish goes up
over Behrampada, another
one buys in.

The newscaster is blonde, and
wears a necklace with
shiny stones.

A woman walks a treadmill,
counting out her steps
in front of five large screens.

Ninety-nine ways to listen to a lie.
Ninety-nine ways to scream.

# Screen

Smokescreen. A quiet street.
The men are hiding there.

Snowscreen. Nails blue with
cold. Faces underlit.

Screen. A graveyard for small flies.
The road tumbles by.

Sunscreen. Slapped on pale legs,
lit to turquoise by the water.

Screen. On the bed, a still hand.
The nurse goes in and out.

Screen. Rumpled underclothes
and tangled wires on the X-ray machine.

Screen. Another veil.
Behind it, her dark face.

Screen. The girl's long hair.
Her nervous fingers.

Screen. Here I am, showing
you the truth on ninety-nine channels.

Screen. Cover this.
Hide this. Let me pass,

I don't want to see
this.

# Ends of the earth

We pass languages
we have no key to,
no shared construction,
no root back to Latin
or to Sanskrit.

But the street is rubbing
right up against us,
talking loudly.
Even if we had doors,
nothing would keep
the other out.

The world is with us
too much. Without
translation the grass is orange
here, that man's carefully parted hair
is green, these people
are dressed
in illuminated neon signs
and birds are coming out
of their mouths instead of words.

Getting and spending,
ending and forgetting,
our powers laid waste.

# Bombay, Mumbai

You wear two names
like scaffolding, your smile held on
with bamboo sticks and sellotape
and string.

Salt swoops in on a sea-wind
and eats you bite by bite,
making sounds like seagulls.
Paint, plaster, brick,
your lovely polished skin
gives in, peels and cracks,
but you fight back,
I am like that only,
you say, and toss your head.

White ants turn
your soul to diamond dust,
flood water slaps
at your glossy mouth, and you
smile back. You leave
doors open.
Absolution slides through the walls
of your heart.

You fall apart.
You make yourself again,
and shrug, I am like that only.

Which other city hands out
two different calling cards

one with the left hand,
the other with the right?

# Anarkali, Lahore

You passed at the very edge of my eye.
Before I could turn you were gone,
but the disturbance in the air
left by your shadow betrayed you.

When I hear your name,
the surge in my blood reminds me
who you were. Anklets like rain,
the sound of your shadow changes everything.

I hear the rumour in the watercourses
of Shalimar, confirmed
by the guilty intake of breath
in the breasts of the Badshahi mosque,
the lover's sigh, the sideways glance,
your shadow caught in these thirsting lanes.

Anarkali you are here in the pomegranate blossom
when the hand touches the forehead and the heart
with the stain of the first love lost,
the absent friend. Lahore you live on
in the shadow of doomed romance.

You have been used and loved, guide, muse,
dancing girl, admired and sighed over,
serenaded. Nothing in you is quite sacred,
or quite profane. You are singing Faiz,
your rhythm is Iqbal.
Poets are the currency
you toss out to the crowd,
not one of us too proud to take
the wine from your mouth
and turn it into a song
we can pass off as our own,
in our throats your shadow.

They were whispering in the bazaar
that you have taken a lover.
This is a lie.
I know there are at least a thousand
who sigh for you, you are the mist in the eye
of the grand old men in Delhi, the grace in the wrist
of the Bombay women,
the girls with faces I recognise
from Southall to San Francisco to Hong Kong.
Your shadow is breathing inside them all.

They say your name. I see it
happen again and again, the catch
in the throat, the hook in the soul,
your shadow altering the climate in our hearts.

# Samarkand
*(for Monika and Charles Correa)*


I ask if he can find the way to
Samarkand, where they sell
in the market the sweetest
melon in the world.
He nods.

I tasted it only once,
I tell him, the one
my friends brought back
by a circuitous route,
Samarkand, Frankfurt, Delhi,
Bombay, the fruit ripening
in transit halls and departure lounges
along the way, growing harder
to carry, heavier
and heavier with juice.

It was my birthday, so
I put a candle in, brought
it out after dinner to the table
where it glowed like the gem
of the east, the pearl of the world,
until we cut it through
its deep cold heart.
The juice burst in our mouths
and we became a part
of its singing,
the poem that ripened
inside the skin.

The mad mogul driver nods again,
as if he hears and understands.

He is willing enough to try
but somehow loses the way
and never finds the city
at the crossroads of the world,
never reaches the river Zarafshan.

# Flag

On a long seashore
otherwise empty
two men are staggering
out of the sea

holding up as best they can
a giant flag.

The engine sputters.
This has caught the driver's eye.

They are struggling
against the sand and wind and rain.

We don't know where they are heading
and they do not look up to see us,
hampered as they are by flapping
cloth.

Wet clothes, wet flag.

A star? A slash of colour,
a flourish.

We cannot see
which country it belongs to.

in the generous heart
of Al Mutamid's city

fragrant, owned by no-one

# Seville

In broad daylight, out
on the road, shameless,
flaunting their true colours
to the open air, following no code,

not nicely dressed in plastic
wrap in supermarket bins,
with proper marks and labels
to cover naked skin

not bought or sold or
paid for at beeping tills,
taken home in plastic bags,
accounted for in lists and bills,

these oranges here are flagrant,
open to the public stare,
on a tree in the generous heart
of Al Mutamid's city

fragrant,
owned by no one.

Not you again

she says

# Cashier Number Three

We struggle at the petrol pump
with the unfamiliarity of filling up

and counting out our foreign coins.
Cyclops has nothing in his hand

or pockets, which are ragged, empty things
as befits a media king.

At the bank, the god in the wall
is unresponsive to my offerings

rejects my password. No plastic flowers,
no incense, no bells will yield a blessing.

So inside to exchange
my dodgy currency.
We join the queue.

*Cashier Number Three.*

Cashier Number Three
looks hard at me,
sees over my shoulder his

one baleful eye. Sighs.
Not you again, she says

# He looks for something

The mad driver tells me
it's time to go to Glasgow.

He looks at me sideways.
I once lost something there, he says.

The rickshaw makes it
over the bridge, where once years ago
Leslie gave me an orange lollipop,

through Eglinton Toll where
Sheila and I stopped at Elizabeth's
and bought toffee apples,

rolls through a red light
at Albert Road, past
Deirdre's house and Dundee cake,

turns into Pollokshields,
past the bus stop, the church
and the sweetie-shop,

parma violets, liquorice,
tablet, aniseed balls,
the scene of a shoplifting,

struggles up the hill at Bruce Road
where the boy from Cyprus lived
with his edible golden skin.

The rickshaw starts limping,
it can't take our weight.
I have to get out.

It occurs to me to ask him, So
you have an International
Driver's Licence?

He snorts.

While I'm asleep at the B&B
(Sheila, Deirdre, Leslie, the Cypriot
long gone)

he's out blowing his horn
all over town, blind as a bat,
looking for the thing he says he lost.

## Tomorrow

Tomorrow I will pierce my navel,
drive hoops through my ears,
and hang chains on my nipples.

Tomorrow my hair will be spiked
and my boots nailed, and my breasts
will be brass
and I will act out of all kinds
of spite.

Tomorrow I will scowl at babies
and make them cry and run
on fat legs away from me.
I will elbow the mothers
and steal trolleys from the
supermarket.

But today.
Today let me just
live through this rickshaw ride.

# In Case of Emergency

Round a corner on two wheels,
too fast. If there is a crash

and they get round to me
they'll look at the heap of clothes

spilled out in the middle
of the road,

and try to work out what to do.
On the double yellow line

they'll find one shoe.

My handbag, split.

The world
will tumble out

on to the road,
a ticket for the tube

Zone 1, from Farringdon
and an entry pass

to Lascaux, a slip from
a peage at Chartres

a ticket for a ferry crossing
from the Gateway of India

to Alibagh,
a receipt for potatoes

I bought in Cairo,
and a page of newspaper

torn out in Tokyo
a photograph, a piece of tissue.

They'll stand there,
considering what to do.

'Anything?'
'Not a clue.'

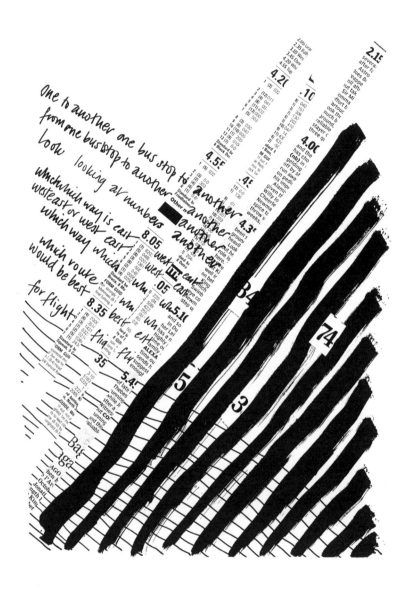

# Bus stop

In Philadelphia or Boston, no sight
or sign to tell me which

I manage to get out
in fright

away from the one-eyed
driver and run

from one bus stop to another,
looking at numbers

and destinations, knowing
nothing of where I am,

which way is east or west
which road would be best

for flight.

The timetable for the night
bus is written in code.

The only other person I can find
to ask is an old woman

at the stop, who jumps
when I speak

to her, then looks up
hopefully with one clear eye

and asks, Can you
take me home?

# Myth

The books promised paradise. A taxi-driver
pointed out the way, past
the traffic-lights, beyond the billboards,
second right. We hoped
we might soon see the tops of trees
haloed in ethereal light.

Not this. Not this.
The everyday. These giant screens
hoisted at street-corners, making
noisy promises. These flags
drifting through the avenues, looking
for a place to settle. Thin
plastic bags puffed up with empty air.

No paradise, this, where lost
souls cry in mobile phones.
A curtain shifts. I freeze.
I have strayed into unknown myths,
every shape a threat.
I shield my eyes, hold up the mirror
to reveal the shrouded enemy. The frost
of my own breath mists the glass

and clears to show
no demon, no terror, no forked tongue,
no head of hissing snakes,
no can of worms, but

only the face I know,
my neighbour, my sister.

The grace of the familiar,
The blessed.
The everyday.

# Smithfield Market

Skittering rickety round the corner
from Blackfriars towards the Market
the rickshaw driver pump
pump pumping at his horn
comes face to face with

a unicorn.

The engine dies. Dead quiet
next to the meat lorries marked L E Jones
the creature lifts its throat
and tilts its head. I could swear
it has been waiting years
right here for us. Mad driver. Lost rider.

Nothing to warn

us that the other world
would have silver eyes, shine
straight into our faces
and take us out of ourselves
so completely that we feel,
in this moment, wrenched
from a womb of rattling tin

untorn.

# Holding my breath

The mist of my breath
slides off the angled mirror
to reveal your face.

* * *

All night, my face next
to your mouth, I hold my breath,
listening to yours.

* * *

A circus of stars,
your dreams a trapeze, faces
lift like mirrored moons.

* * *

Hung above your sleep,
Low moon on your horizon,
My heart grows immense.

# Half-breath

The engine gasps, stops. We walk,
clinking our thoughts like coins
that are no longer currency. I have done
nothing to be proud of. No
words of mine can change the clocks.
You are not healed.

But the morning feels itself
released from sound
into a crystal arc of sky,
the world revealed, fresh-grown
out of water, the first garden,
and people come out blinking in the light.

As we pass a stranger smiles,
Sunlight stretches out to stroke
your head and the city glitters
in your hair.

Out of season, crocuses try
to break through frozen ground.
Halfway, on this half-formed day,

my heart feels forgiven.

# Halfway

We ride frequented motorways
where trucks snort past
and leave the rickshaw flapping
in their wake.

We make our way through city centres,
down high streets and round squares
where people point at us, the decorations,
tinsel, bumper painting,
and smile or stare.

On coastal roads and highways,
we pass the singing crowds,
a running girl with ribbons streaming
from her hair, the architect
struggling with the weight
of a melon that could only have come
from Samarkand,
Men stumble from the sea
with giant flags, wind-whipped.
Children climb over a stone head. Whose?

We navigate this fractured time
consulting ancient maps,
overtaking on the autoroutes
the unicorn, the poet king.

Halfway home or halfway gone,
we have grown accustomed now
to travelling on the faultline

of daily miracles.